Jane Goodall

Jennifer Strand

abdopublishing.com

Published by Abdo Zoom™, PO Box 398166, Minneapolis, Minnesota 55439. Copyright © 2017 by Abdo Consulting Group, Inc. International copyrights reserved in all countries. No part of this book may be reproduced in any form without written permission from the publisher. Abdo Zoom™ is a trademark and logo of Abdo Consulting Group, Inc.

Printed in the United States of America, North Mankato, Minnesota
072016
092016

THIS BOOK CONTAINS
RECYCLED MATERIALS

Cover Photo: Kathy Willens/AP Images
Interior Photos: Kathy Willens/AP Images, 1; Michael Nichols/National Geographic Creative, 5; iStockphoto, 6, 8–9; CBS Photo Archive/Getty Images, 7; Gerry Ellis/Minden Pictures/Newscom, 9; Everett Collection/Newscom, 10; Marques Photography/iStockphoto, 11; Penelope Breese/Liaison/Getty Images, 12–13; AP Images, 14; Jeryl Tan/iStockphoto, 15; Sean Kilpatrick/The Canadian Press/AP Images, 17; Stefan Rousseau/EPA/Newscom, 18; Stephen Robinson/NHPA/Photoshot/Newscom, 19

Editor: Brienna Rossiter
Series Designer: Madeline Berger
Art Direction: Dorothy Toth

Publisher's Cataloging-in-Publication Data
Names: Strand, Jennifer, author.
Title: Jane Goodall / by Jennifer Strand.
Description: Minneapolis, MN : Abdo Zoom, [2017] | Series: Great women |
    Includes bibliographical references and index.
Identifiers: LCCN 2016941355 | ISBN 9781680792218 (lib. bdg.) |
    ISBN 9781680793895 (ebook) | 9781680794786 (Read-to-me ebook)
Subjects: LCSH: Goodall, Jane, 1934-- Juvenile literature. | Primatologists--
    England--Biography--Juvenile literature. | Women primatologists--England-
    Biography--Juvenile literature. | Chimpanzees--Tanzania--Gombe National
    Park--Juvenile literature.
Classification: DDC 590.92 [B]--dc23
LC record available at http://lccn.loc.gov/2016941355

Table of Contents

Introduction

Jane Goodall is a famous scientist.
She studies chimpanzees.
She also works to protect animals.

Early Life

Jane was born on April 3, 1934. She lived in London, England.

Jane had many pets.
She wanted to study animals.

Leader

Goodall dreamed of living in Africa. In 1957 she went to Kenya.

She visited a friend's farm there.

In Africa she met Louis Leakey.
He was an **archaeologist**.

She helped him dig for **fossils**.

History Maker

Leakey asked Goodall to study chimpanzees.

She lived with the
chimps in the forest.
She watched them
for many days.

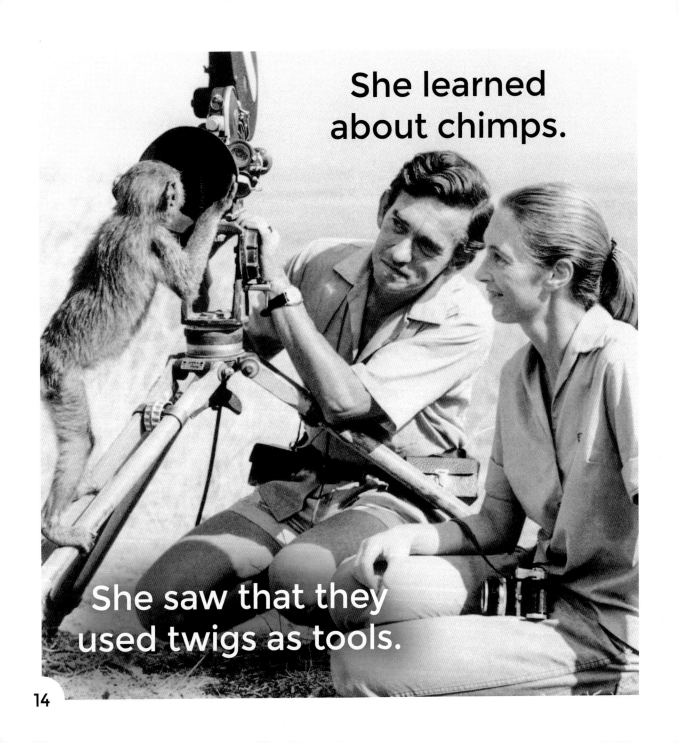

She learned
about chimps.

She saw that they
used twigs as tools.

This was important. Scientists had thought only humans used tools.

Legacy

Goodall works to help animals. In 1977 she started the Jane Goodall Institute.

It protects apes and their habitats.

Goodall has won many awards for her **research**.

She continues to work
to save animals.

Quick Stats

Jane Goodall

Born: April 3, 1934

Birthplace: London, England

Known For: Goodall is a scientist. She studies chimpanzees. She also works to protect apes and other animals.

Key Dates

1934: Valerie Jane Morris-Goodall is born on April 3.

1957: Goodall starts working for Louis Leakey.

1960: Goodall begins studying chimpanzees.

1977: Goodall founds the Jane Goodall Institute.

1991: Goodall starts Roots & Shoots to help kids care for the earth.

2002: Goodall is named a United Nations Messenger of Peace.

Glossary

ape - a large animal that is similar to monkeys and humans.

archaeologist - a person who studies objects left behind by humans who lived long ago.

fossils - the remains of plants or animals from a long time ago.

habitat - a place where a living thing is naturally found.

research - careful study to learn new facts or solve a problem.

Booklinks

For more information
on **Jane Goodall**, please visit
booklinks.abdopublishing.com

Zoom In on Biographies!

Learn even more with the Abdo Zoom
Biographies database. Check out
abdozoom.com for more information.

Index